AF270192

1 TIMOTHY– HEBREWS

1 TIMOTHY– HEBREWS

Rob Wynalda, Joel R. Beeke, and Paul M. Smalley

REFORMATION HERITAGE BOOKS

Grand Rapids, Michigan

Reformation Heritage Books
3070 29th St. SE
Grand Rapids, MI 49512
616-977-0889
orders@heritagebooks.org
www.heritagebooks.org

25 26 27 28 29 30/11 10 9 8 7 6 5 4 3 2

ISBN 979-8-88686-171-6

PREFACE

In Deuteronomy 17, Moses leaves final instructions concerning the future of Israel. As a prophet of God, he foretells that Israel will set a king over the nation (v. 14). This king must be an Israelite, not a foreigner (v. 15), and is forbidden to do certain things (vv. 16–17). In verse 18, Moses transitions to what the king should do. The king is commanded not to simply acquire a copy of the law (the entire book of Deuteronomy), but to handwrite his own copy of the law. The purpose was so that he would read it, fear the Lord, obey, avoid pride, not deviate, and enjoy a long reign (vv. 19–20; cf. Prov. 4:20–27).

More than three thousand years later, modern educators have discovered that students who write out notes by hand have a much higher retention rate than those who simply hear or visually read the information. Apparently, God knew this to be true for the kings of Israel also.

This series of books, known as The Bible Journal, was born from the insight found in Deuteronomy 17:18. Your Bible Journal gives you the opportunity to write out your own copy of a portion of the Holy Scriptures, just as the ancient kings of Israel were instructed to do. Writing out the words of the Bible helps a person to engage the Word of God by slowing down the process of reading the text. Writing answers to the discussion questions also helps you to thoughtfully engage the text. Furthermore, by completing a journal, you leave a legacy to pass on to future generations your insights and personal applications of the text (Deut. 6:6–9; Ps. 78:4–7).

To prepare you to meditate on this portion of the Holy Scriptures, we include an introduction to the book of the Bible to help you understand more thoroughly the Bible book you are about to write out in full. Study Questions and Devotional Reflections have been added after the blank pages set aside for copying each chapter of God's Word. The Study Questions focus on individual verses to keep you thinking about what you are writing, and the Devotional Reflections are designed to help you focus on a few of the major takeaways for your practical Christian life that each Bible chapter provides. We wish to thank Reformation Heritage Books for allowing us to use material drawn from *The Reformation Heritage KJV Study Bible* for the Bible Introduction material and for the Devotional Reflections. The Study Questions have been written by the authors of *The Bible Journal*. Thus, The Bible Journal walks you through a process of getting acquainted with a book of the Bible, copying a chapter by hand, reflecting on the meaning and application of that chapter, and then repeating the process for the next chapter. Families, friends, and small groups can work through a journal together, discussing their meditations for mutual edification as guided by the discussion questions.

The mass production of the Bible since the invention of the printing press has greatly blessed the world. However, there is also great benefit for Bible readers of all ages in following the Deuteronomy 17:18 principle and producing your own handwritten copy of the text.

May God richly bless you in writing and learning His Word through The Bible Journal (Rom. 1:16).

—Rob Wynalda, Joel R. Beeke, and Paul M. Smalley

Introduction to the Book of
1 TIMOTHY

AUTHORSHIP: According to the salutation we find in 1:1, the author of 1 Timothy is the apostle Paul. Paul attests to the fact that he used to be "a blasphemer, and a persecutor" (v. 13), but that the grace of God "was exceeding abundant" (v. 14) and that Christ Jesus placed him "into the ministry" (v. 12)—all things we know of Paul's life. The early church unanimously held to Pauline authorship for this epistle.

The addressee is Timothy. Since it is addressed to an individual and not a whole church, and deals with issues relating to the character and conduct of a minister, it has become known as a pastoral epistle (along with 2 Timothy and Titus). Timothy was one of the best known of Paul's companions and fellow-laborers (Acts 16:1–3; 19:22; 1 Cor. 4:17; 2 Cor. 1:1; Phil. 1:1; etc.). We know from the biblical record that Timothy was much younger than Paul (1 Tim. 4:12). He had been an elder in Ephesus continuing the work of Paul throughout Asia Minor of building up the church (cf. Rom. 15:19). Timothy's mother was Jewish and his father was a Greek—which meant that Timothy was both raised in the Scriptures and had a high status in society (Acts 16:1). He was one of Paul's converts, as Paul called him his "own son in the faith" (1 Tim. 1:2).

Timothy was a resident and probably a native of Lystra, one of the cities Paul visited during his first missionary journey (Acts 14:6). Later Paul refers to the things he suffered in Lystra, saying that Timothy is fully aware of what he endured (2 Tim. 3:10–11). Apparently Timothy's mother, Eunice, and his grandmother, Lois, had first come to faith and subsequently Timothy did also.

At the time of Paul's second missionary journey, and upon revisiting Lystra (Acts 16:1), Paul requested Timothy to become one of his associates. Since Timothy was the son of a Jewish woman, and realizing the need for him to gain access to the Jews, Paul circumcised Timothy (Acts 16:3). Timothy was sent on assignments to organize churches and preach the gospel. To the very end of his life Paul was greatly comforted by Timothy (2 Tim. 4:9, 21).

1

DATE: Scholars agree that the circumstances mentioned in the two epistles of Paul to Timothy do not fit any scenario in the book of Acts. This leads us to conclude that these two epistles were written at a later date, after Paul had been released from his two-year imprisonment at Rome. The book of Acts ends with Paul undergoing house arrest. During that time he was free to do his work, receive visitors, and preach the gospel.

The personal circumstances of Paul, as reflected in 1 Timothy, were different. He was in Macedonia and had requested Timothy to remain in Ephesus (1:3). In 2 Timothy, Paul was back in prison and had been forsaken. Only Luke was with him (2 Tim. 4:11). Paul felt, at that time, as though death was staring him in the face.

All this suggests that Paul was released from his first imprisonment at Rome, allowing him to conduct missionary travels. After being arrested a second time and brought to Rome, he was, according to church history, put on trial and finally executed (AD 67). The conclusion is drawn that 1 Timothy was written some time after his first imprisonment and probably from Macedonia (perhaps Philippi).

THEME: Contending for the Christian faith and establishing the Christian church.

PURPOSE: Paul wrote to encourage Timothy to remain faithful to the gospel and to organize the church according to the apostolic pattern for the church.

SYNOPSIS

The Contribution of 1 Timothy to Redemptive Revelation
Paul encourages Timothy, young and timid as he appears to have been at this time, to fulfill his ministry with boldness and perseverance. Timothy must stand fast in the face of difficulties. There are dangers from within the church as well as from without. A dangerous group of Judaizers were attempting to impose Jewish legalism upon the newly founded church (1:9), militating against the doctrine of free grace. There were heretics who were promoting "doctrines of devils," that espoused a philosophical dualism (4:1). This dualism apparently taught that there were two supreme beings, one working for the good and the other working for evil. Paul instructs Timothy to lift up the one,

only, and supreme Creator God. Satan is a mere fallen creature who, though bent on ruin and deformed by pride (3:6), is subject to God.

Timothy must likewise resist those who teach doctrines underestimating the value of the body and denying the physical resurrection of the dead. Such forbid marriage and emphasize abstention from certain foods (4:3). As a minister in Ephesus, Timothy must oppose all these different heresies and promote the "sound doctrine" (1:10).

Paul also shows Timothy how the church ought to be properly organized. Some of the apostles were already being taken away by death. Paul explains here to Timothy directions for public worship (ch. 2) and how the churches should be organized (ch. 3) after the oversight of the apostles was no longer available other than in their divinely written testimony.

OUTLINE

I. Salutation (1:1–2)

II. The Purity of the Gospel (1:3–20)
    A. Warning against Heretics Promoting Jewish Legalism (1:3–11)
    B. The Proclamation of the Gospel Entrusted to Paul (1:12–17)
    C. Timothy Encouraged to Be Faithful to the Gospel (1:18–20)

III. Ordinances and Worship (2:1–3:16)
    A. Direction for Prayer by Men in Worship Services (2:1–8)
    B. Women Are to Pray Along Silently (2:9–15)
    C. Qualifications for Elders (3:1–7)
    D. Qualifications for Deacons (3:8–13)
    E. Calling of the Church to Uphold Truth (3:14–16)

IV. Practical Encouragements for Ministers (4:1–6:16)
    A. Warning against Heresies Still to Come (4:1–5)
    B. Timothy Called to Be a Godly Example (4:6–16)
    C. How to Admonish Church Members (5:1–2)
    D. How to Counsel Widows (5:3–16)
    E. How to Counsel Elders (5:17–25)
    F. How to Counsel Slaves (6:1–2)
    G. Godliness Is Great Gain (6:3–10)
    H. Encouragement to Timothy to Be Faithful (6:11–16)

V. Final Exhortations (6:17–21)
    A. How to Counsel the Rich (6:17–19)
    B. Final Encouragement to Timothy to Be Faithful (6:20–21)

Notes

1

2

3

4

5

6

7

Notes

8

9

10

11

12

13

14

Notes

15

16

17

18

19

20

STUDY QUESTIONS

1. Verse 2: What does Paul call Timothy? What does that say about their relationship?

2. Verse 5: What is the aim of true biblical instruction?

3. Verses 9–10: What kinds of people does the law rebuke? Which of the Ten Commandments are these sinners violating (Ex. 20:1–17)?

4. Verses 13–14: How does Paul describe his conversion?

5. Verse 15: What "faithful saying" does Paul repeat here?

6. Verse 17: What attributes of God are presented in this doxology?

7. Verse 20: What had Paul done with these false teachers (1 Cor. 5:5)?

DEVOTIONAL REFLECTIONS

1. Note Paul's reference to "God our Saviour" in verse 1. Paul uses this designation also in 1 Timothy 2:3 and 4:10. The Son of God merited salvation for His people, dying on the cross and rising on the third day. But the source of salvation rests in God, the Father. Paul frequently ascribes man's salvation to God (Rom. 8:32; 1 Cor. 1:21; Eph. 2:4–5; etc.). Verse 15 beautifully mentions Christ's saving work. To be saved means also that God gives man the richest blessings: to declare that man is righteous in the sight of God (Isa. 1:18; Rom. 3:24), is placed in the freedom of God's children (Rom. 8:2; 2 Cor. 3:17; Gal. 5:1), and receives everlasting life (John 11:25–26; Eph. 2:5; Rev. 22:5).

2. Note also Paul's reference in verse 1 to the "Lord Jesus Christ…our hope." He is not only the One who gives hope, but Christ Himself is the hope of His people. He is the foundation of Christian hope, for Christ earned that hope when He laid down His life as a ransom for sin. This is a source of unspeakable comfort. Christ is also the door of hope. One enters into a life of hope through Him. He is the only access to God. We, unworthy guilty sinners, can only have access to God through Christ. Christ is also the life of hope. One can only live in true hope through Christ. Without it there is no comfort or perspective for the future.

3. Verse 8 speaks of the law of God, which is good and is to be used lawfully. How do we use the law lawfully? There are various uses of the law. It functions as a restraint, working in people's consciences and keeping them from committing certain sins (Rom. 2:15). The law of God reveals to us our sins (Rom. 3:20), which need to be washed in the blood of Christ. Finally, the law is also a guide to lead us through life (Pss. 19:8; 119:98; Rom. 7:22).

Notes

1

2

3

4

5

6

7

8

9

10

11

12

13

14

15

STUDY QUESTIONS

1. Verses 1–2: What is the duty of Christians to their civil leaders?

2. Verses 4–6: Why should Christians pray for the salvation of all kinds of people?

3. Verses 9–10: How should women make themselves beautiful?

4. Verse 12: What does Paul forbid women to do?

5. Verses 13–14: What reasons does Paul give for forbidding women to do that?

DEVOTIONAL REFLECTIONS

1. Notice Paul's emphasis on prayer. Christian prayer has a tremendous impact upon the surrounding environment. God answers prayer. The apostle often stresses the importance of prayer, requesting prayer for himself and for the work in God's kingdom (Eph. 6:18–19; Heb. 13:18). In Acts 6:4 the apostles testify that they should give themselves to prayer. In Acts 12:5 the church prayed without ceasing for Peter who had been put in prison. The Lord Jesus stresses the importance of personal and corporate prayer (Matt. 6:6; 7:7–8; Mark 9:25). Let us pray for individuals by name, asking for God's grace upon their lives.

2. Let us realize the basic truth that there is one Mediator between God and men (v. 5). This counts for all men everywhere. It is only in Christ that man can be reconciled to God. That is because Jesus Christ paid the ransom. He gave Himself as a payment for sin. Outside of Christ there is no reconciliation and no propitiation. This is why no one other than Christ can ever mediate between God and man. As God, Christ was able to endure the eternal wrath of God. As man, Christ fulfilled the law perfectly for His people. Now, in Christ men can come to God in faith, and this faith does not put to shame.

Notes

1

2

3

4

5

6

7

8

Notes

9

10

11

12

13

14

15

Notes

16

STUDY QUESTIONS

1. Verse 1: What is a "bishop" or "overseer" (see Acts 20:17–35, esp. v. 28)?

2. Verse 2: What is the basic moral qualification for this office, listed first by Paul (Titus 1:7)? What gift or ability is needed to perform it (Titus 1:9)?

3. Verse 8: What is a "deacon" (Phil. 1:1; see Acts 6:1–7)?

4. Verse 13: What blessings do faithful deacons receive from the Lord?

5. Verse 15: What is the church called? How does that show us why it is important to follow God's instructions of how to behave in the church?

6. Verse 16: What does it mean that God "was manifest in the flesh" (see John 1:14)?

DEVOTIONAL REFLECTIONS

1. Paul describes here the requirements of an office bearer. The reference to the office as a "good work" in verse 1 shows that Paul has a high regard for the office. This implies that it is an excellent and honorable work. Nevertheless we know from early church history that in those days serving in the office was also a sacrifice. Repeatedly persecution would rage with painful consequences. False teachers did their utmost to undermine the truth. The cares of the congregation were many (2 Cor. 11:27–28). Still today, serving in the office is a sacrifice. There is the sacrifice of time, ease, and energy. At times there will be suffering because of hardships and ill-spoken words against the office bearer. At times one's name will even be slandered for the sake of being faithful to one's calling. But let it then be realized, that it is still a "good work" worthy of performing.

2. One of the qualifications Paul gives for an overseer is that he must be "blameless" (v. 2). We understand that to mean that he is to be beyond reproach and to have a good name both within and beyond the church. However, let us also realize that at heart no office bearer is "blameless" for all have sinned and come short of the glory of God (Rom. 3:23). Therefore ultimately the office bearer can only be "blameless" in Christ. Christ justifies and cleanses from sin. Every office bearer has reason to consider himself unworthy and not beyond reproach. Without undermining the need to be godly in one's conduct, let us also realize that every office bearer needs to be clothed with the righteousness of Christ. This is the only way he can be truly blameless.

3. It seems that within churches pastors are often under attack. The Evil One will try to render a pastor's work useless by leading him to fall into sin, for if the pastor falls, many in the congregation will stumble with him and the church will be in disarray. This is true not only for the pastors but also for the elders and the deacons. They are called to have oversight of the flock and therefore they must first have oversight over themselves in the privacy of their own homes and lives. This fact ought to stir up congregants to pray for those who are office bearers over them and to be cautious lest they unduly grumble (Numbers 12).

Notes

1

2

3

4

5

6

7

8

Notes

9

10

11

12

13

14

15

16

STUDY QUESTIONS

1. Verse 1: What warning did the Holy Spirit give about the latter times?

2. Verses 4–5: Why is it wrong, even demonic (v. 1), to treat God's creations like marriage and food as if they were bad? How can we properly use these gifts from God?

3. Verses 7–8: Why is spiritual exercise more valuable than physical exercise?

4. Verse 12: How can a young minister win the respect of believers?

5. Verse 16: To what must a minister give careful attention? Why?

DEVOTIONAL REFLECTIONS

1. Paul encourages Timothy to exercise himself "unto godliness" (v. 7). One's fruitfulness in the service of the Lord depends on it. It promotes an increase in the knowledge of sin and of the necessity and preciousness of Christ. This exercise as such will remain hidden but the effects of it will be public. It is the calling and the duty of God's children to be diligent in reading the Scriptures and in seeking the Lord in personal, private prayer. Meditating on the mysteries of godliness as revealed to us in God's Word and praying over this will cultivate a rich fruit in the life of a Christian. If one wishes to experience more of the love of Christ and be led deeper into a life of communion with Christ, one will need to have daily secret spiritual exercises. For "thy Father which seeth in secret shall reward thee openly" (Matt. 6:6).

2. Paul encourages Timothy to read the Scriptures with attention (v. 13). If we are to be godly in this crooked world, we will need to diligently read the Scriptures and meditate on their doctrines, making applications to daily life in the way of pointed exhortations. Without them, our lives and worship will suffer detrimentally.

Notes

Chapter 5

1

2

3

4

5

6

7

8

Notes

9

10

11

12

13

14

Notes

15

16

17

18

19

20

21

Notes

22

23

24

25

STUDY QUESTIONS

1. Verses 1–2: How should a believer relate to other kinds of people in church?

2. Verse 4: Who has the primary responsibility to care for needy widows (vv. 8, 16)?

3. Verses 9–10: What kind of widows should the church help to support?

4. Verse 14: What is Paul's instruction for younger widows?

5. Verses 17–18: What should the church do for elders who labor in the ministry of the Word?

6. Verses 19–20: How should the church respond to accusations against elders?

7. Verse 22: What caution should ministers exercise in ordaining men to office?

8. Verses 24–25: What does Paul say about different people's sins and good works?

DEVOTIONAL REFLECTIONS

1. Paul instructs Timothy how to deal with various age categories in the congregation. He refers to fathers, mothers, younger men, and women. This shows the importance of family life. In our society indifference toward family members is increasing. The church ought to reflect brotherly love, mutual respect, and an attitude of esteeming the other higher than oneself. In this way the church will be a witness in this world of Christian love and faithfulness.

2. Timothy is called to assess people's lives. In this regard the fruits will show who people are. We cannot judge the inward attitude, but may only listen to the testimony and observe the outward walk of life. It may be that we will see that much is lacking in our congregation. The church needs to strike a balance between showing forbearance to weak members while encouraging improvement and publicly admonishing sin. All this must be accompanied with urgent prayer for the outpouring of God's Spirit in the midst of the congregation.

Notes

1

2

3

4

5

6

Notes

7

8

9

10

11

12

13

Notes

14

15

16

17

18

19

Notes

20

21

STUDY QUESTIONS

1. Verse 2: How should Christian servants treat Christian masters? Why?

2. Verses 3–5: What does Paul say about false and divisive teachers?

3. Verses 6–8: What is the great gain we can receive in this life?

4. Verse 11: What should a man of God flee (vv. 9–10)? What should he pursue?

5. Verses 15–16: What titles and attributes does this doxology ascribe to the Lord?

6. Verses 17–19: What instruction should ministers give to the rich?

7. Verse 20: What must a minister keep or guard? What must he avoid?

DEVOTIONAL REFLECTIONS

1. Paul gives directions for slaves and masters. As such Paul does not outlaw slavery, but provides a framework within which masters and their slaves must operate on the basis of mutual respect, love, and trust. Thereby in reality the institution of slavery is undermined. In our days slave trade is forbidden, but pride and antagonism against other people, races, and those of a different social status, as well as foreigners, is deeply ingrained in the human heart. Paul points out to us the Christian attitude of love, respect, and care toward all people.

2. This passage also teaches us the need not to be attached to the material blessings of this world. This world is transient. Only the salvation of the Lord Jesus Christ remains forever. We may be grateful for the many blessings of this world and use them, but at the same time realize the needs of others, alleviating them where we can. Let us use this life as a preparation for eternal life.

Introduction to the Book of
2 TIMOTHY

AUTHORSHIP: According to the salutation, Paul wrote the epistle of 2 Timothy (1:1) with the apostolic authority he received from Christ, being sent by God (v. 11). The author relates the struggle of his personal circumstances: he was in prison and had already been on trial (4:16). He knew that his death was imminent (4:6), and he had "fought a good fight" and finished his course (4:7). Early church testimonies of those adhering to the orthodox faith are unanimous in stating that the apostle Paul was the author of 2 Timothy. Church leaders at the end of the first century quote from 2 Timothy, which shows that this epistle has apostolic authority.

Like 1 Timothy, this epistle was written "To Timothy, my dearly beloved son" (1:2). Timothy played an important role in the early church and was very special to Paul. He was Paul's spiritual son, probably converted during Paul's first missionary journey. Leaving his native Lystra, he accompanied Paul on his second and third missionary journeys. Paul also sent him to give direction to local churches. He seems to have been a timid person, in need of encouragement (vv. 7–8; 2:1–6).

DATE: Scholars agree that the circumstances mentioned in 1 and 2 Timothy do not reflect any particular scenario in the book of Acts. This leads us to conclude that these two epistles were written at a later date, after Paul had been released from his two-year imprisonment at Rome. Shortly before his imprisonment Paul had been in Troas (4:13), a major city in the northwest of Asia Minor, on the coast of Mysia. Because Paul left his cloak there, it can be assumed that he was there in the summer, and as he desired Timothy to come to him before the winter, we may also assume that Paul has not been in prison for a long time and that it is now fall of that same year. Paul's first imprisonment was a house arrest (Acts 28). This second imprisonment was of a different nature. Paul felt forsaken (2 Tim. 4:16) and Onesiphorus had to search "very diligently" to find out where he was imprisoned (1:17). Historians estimate that Paul was put to death around AD 67. However, the chronology of the closing events of Paul's life is too obscure to be certain what year he wrote this epistle.

THEME: Encouragement in the ministry against hardships and false doctrines.

PURPOSE: Paul writes to encourage Timothy to remain faithful, even as Paul has, in the ministry that has been entrusted to him, that he too might receive the crown of glory.

SYNOPSIS
The Contribution of 2 Timothy to Redemptive Revelation
There appear to be similarities between the two letters written to Timothy. In both, Timothy is encouraged to be strong, to organize church life, and to be alert for false teachers. Although both epistles aim at encouraging Timothy to be faithful to the Lord, however, there are profound differences. The first letter has a more objective and business-like tone, dealing with various issues of organizing and protecting church life. The second is more personal; it is the spiritual legacy of a dying friend and brother in the Lord. Paul longs for Timothy's presence, repeatedly asking him to come and visit him in his imprisonment (4:9, 21).

OUTLINE
I. Salutations and Thanksgiving (1:1–5)
    A. Address of the Epistle (1:1–2)
    B. Thanksgiving to God for Timothy's Faith (1:3–5)

II. Encouragements and Exhortations (1:6–2:13)
    A. Exhortation to Grasp Courage and Not to Be Ashamed of Truth (1:6–11)
    B. Admonition to Hold Fast the Truth (1:12–18)
    C. Encouragement to Endure Hardship in the Ministry (2:1–13)

III. Warnings and Exhortations to Encourage Perseverance (2:14–4:5)
    A. Warnings against Heretics, False Doctrine, and Other Sins (2:14–26)
    B. Warning against Falling Away in the Last Days (3:1–9)
    C. Exhortation to Stand Firm on the Word of God (3:10–17)
    D. Exhortation to Preach the Word of God (4:1–5)

Notes

1

2

3

4

5

6

7

Notes

8

9

10

11

12

13

Notes

14

15

16

17

18

STUDY QUESTIONS

1. Verse 3: What does Paul say about his service to God?

2. Verse 5: What spiritual privilege did Timothy enjoy in his family?

3. Verse 7: What has God not given His children? What has He given them?

4. Verse 9: What does Paul teach about salvation here?

5. Verses 13–14: What must Christians, especially ministers such as Timothy, guard and cherish?

6. Verses 16–18: What does Paul wish for the household of Onesiphorus? Why?

DEVOTIONAL REFLECTIONS

1. Paul reminds Timothy of the deeds of the Lord in the past. He speaks of the faith of Timothy's mother and grandmother and reminds him of the faith Timothy had shown in the past. This is all to encourage Timothy to persevere in the calling God has given him. It is beneficial for our spiritual lives to meditate on the deeds of the Lord in our own lives as well as the lives of loved ones (Ps. 77:11–12).

2. Note how the apostle prays for Timothy day and night. Paul had a high regard for prayer. We see this sprinkled throughout his epistles. Every time he prays, he thinks of Timothy. Paul prayed much, for he believed in God who answers prayer. He realized that God sovereignly incorporates the prayers of His people in His dealings with mankind.

Notes

1

2

3

4

5

6

7

8

9

Notes

10

11

12

13

14

15

16

17

Notes

18

19

20

21

22

23

Notes

24

25

26

STUDY QUESTIONS

1. Verse 2: What must the church do to continue the ministry of the Word?

2. Verses 3–6: What three metaphors does Paul use for the ministry? What does each mean?

3. Verses 9–10: What are some reasons why opposition to the gospel need not discourage us?

4. Verse 12: What promise and warning does this verse contain?

5. Verse 15: What should be the holy ambition of every teacher of God's Word?

6. Verses 17–18: What heresy did these men teach? What effect did it have?

7. Verses 20–21: What can we learn from this parable of vessels in a house (v. 22)?

8. Verse 24: How should a minister act toward people, including unbelievers?

9. Verses 25–26: How does this show that sinners cannot save themselves?

DEVOTIONAL REFLECTIONS

1. Paul encourages Timothy in verse 3 to endure difficulty as a good soldier of Jesus Christ. To some extent hardships and difficulties will be the share of all who are called to be a witness of the Lord Jesus Christ. Timothy, as a minister of the gospel, had to reckon with these hardships and not be surprised when they occurred. Likewise now all office bearers must count on hardships in their official work. But also God's children, as they are called to be witnesses of the Lord Jesus Christ, must reckon with scorn, tribulation, and other hardships as they witness from the Word of God.

2. Timothy must strive lawfully (v. 5). What does this mean? An office bearer should be honest and upright. He may not be proud or strive for glory from men. He should not be discouraged by hardships. He should not waste his energy. He should not consider himself to be indispensable. He should be willing to share the work with others and not promote himself. He must submit himself to proper church oversight, especially regarding the preaching of God's Word. He must show willingness to learn from others.

3. In verse 25 the purpose of all pastoral work toward those that oppose the gospel is stated. The word used there in the original is stronger than repentance. It is conversion, which implies a total change in mental and moral outlook on life. It leads to a radical change of one's attitude and conduct. Such change is not the fruit of man's persuasion but is always worked by God's Spirit, as a gift of God. Let us be humble when we know this change of life. Let our need for conversion drive us to hope in the Lord. Be careful not to grieve God's Spirit but in humility expect His working in your life.

Notes

1

2

3

4

5

6

7

8

Notes

9

10

11

12

13

14

15

Notes

16

17

STUDY QUESTIONS

1. Verses 2–4: What do these people love? Who do they not love? Who else?

2. Verse 6: Who do false teachers seek to exploit?

3. Verses 10–11: How is Paul an example from whom we can learn much?

4. Verse 12: What should godly people expect to happen to them?

5. Verse 15: What are the Scriptures able to do, even for children?

6. Verses 16–17: What is special about the Scriptures? How does that make them useful?

DEVOTIONAL REFLECTIONS

1. In verse 8 mention is made of two Egyptian magicians whose names, until now, have not been mentioned in the Bible. God has seen fit to give us their names here. This fact should remind us that God remembers each person's individual name, thoughts, and actions. Though all of humanity forget us, God remembers still. Judgment day will reveal many things history has forgotten. Let us therefore seek to be well grounded in Scripture as the cornerstone of faith.

2. In verse 12 the apostle teaches that all who wish to live godly in Christ will suffer forms of hardship, suffering, and even persecution. They may be despised or even ostracized for the sake of the gospel. All those who wish to live godly should realize this and prepare themselves mentally in advance for such events, so as not to be shocked when they actually take place. By the Spirit's grace, they will then be able to endure such hardships and remain faithful to the Lord.

Notes

1

2

3

4

5

6

7

Notes

8

9

10

11

12

13

14

15

16

Notes

17

18

19

20

21

22

STUDY QUESTIONS

1. Verses 1–2: What is the minister's duty? What should motivate him to do it?

2. Verses 3–4: What makes a minister's work difficult?

3. Verses 7–8: What can Paul say about his life and future reward?

4. Verse 10: Why did Demas desert Paul? How is that a warning to us?

5. Verses 14–15: What did Alexander do? What did Paul call on God to do?

6. Verse 17: How did Paul have the strength to stand alone (v. 16) in his trial?

7. Verse 18: What was Paul's confident hope?

8. Verse 22: What benediction does Paul speak on Timothy? What does this mean?

DEVOTIONAL REFLECTIONS

1. In verse 2 we read that Paul desires Timothy to emphasize doctrine in his teaching. Today doctrine is not viewed as useful and people generally prefer "practical preaching." But a church without doctrine is like a house without a structure or a building without a foundation. The church of the Lord Jesus Christ needs to be instructed in the doctrines of God's Word. Therefore preaching should contain a major focus on the fundamental Christian doctrines, such as those found in the Heidelberg Catechism or the Westminster Shorter Catechism. Parents should instruct their children in these truths.

2. In verse 8 we read of the reward the Lord has set in store for all those who love Him. God's people are called to meditate on the future blessings the Lord shall give to His own. One moment in glory will make all the struggles on earth worthwhile. In the midst of trials and hardships, this is a great impetus to continue the struggle, knowing that their heavenly reward is firm and sure. The future glory of God's people is grounded in Christ's resurrection. The outpouring of the Holy Ghost is a down payment of the full blessing which is still to come.

Introduction to the Book of
TITUS

AUTHORSHIP: Irenaeus in the second century AD ascribed this letter to Paul. Against this, some scholars have argued that the epistles to Titus and Timothy could not have been written by Paul because: (1) their vocabulary and style differ from Paul's other letters, (2) they present a more formal and organized view of the church than Paul held, and (3) early Christians welcomed pseudonymous letters written in the name of a famous leader as an honor to him, not as a form of deceit.

In response, we make the following points: (1) An epistle's style varies according to the author's situation, the person or group to whom he writes, and the scribe to whom he dictates the letter (Rom. 16:22; 1 Cor. 16:21; 2 Thess. 3:17). (2) These epistles do not contradict Paul's view of the church. He organized churches under the oversight of elders and with the ministry of deacons (Acts 14:23; 20:17, 28; Phil. 1:1). (3) Although some ancient apocalyptic writings, sermons, and histories were pseudonymous, it is not true that ancient Christians wrote and welcomed letters under false names. Paul warned against letters falsely claiming to be from him (2 Thess. 2:2), and early church leaders such as Tertullian (c. AD 160–c. 225) and Serapion (d. AD 211) condemned writings that falsely bore the names of apostles. It would be the worse hypocrisy for this author to pretend to be Paul while declaring the "truth" from God who "cannot lie," and warning against "deceivers" (1:1–2, 10).

In the end, we return to the claims of the Bible itself. The author identifies himself as Paul (1:1), refers to Titus as his "own son" in the faith (v. 4), and references how Paul left him in Crete with specific instructions (v. 5). He speaks of his plan to stay the winter at Nicopolis, and urges Titus to visit him there if possible (3:12). Thus this book presents itself as a personal epistle from the apostle to a dear friend and coworker in ministry.

DATE: Perhaps about the same time as 1 Timothy, around AD 62–64, between Paul's first imprisonment at Rome (AD 62) and his imprisonment and execution there (AD 64–67).

THEME: The church should be established through solid leadership and a sober lifestyle of godliness produced by the sound doctrines of election, redemption, and regeneration.

PURPOSE: To encourage a pastor in leading the church to overcome false teaching and mankind's inherent tendency to disorder and wickedness.

SYNOPSIS

The Contribution of Titus to Redemptive Revelation

Titus was the man Paul looked to for the most difficult assignments, such as completing the reformation of doctrine and life in the church at Corinth (2 Cor. 2:12–13; 7:6–7, 13–15; 8:6, 16–17, 23–24; 12:18). The church in Crete, a large Mediterranean island south of the Greek mainland, faced a number of challenges. False teachers sought to divide the church's members with Jewish legalism and traditions (1:10, 14; 3:9–10), perhaps combined with Greek philosophical speculations. The cultural sins characteristic of the Cretans (1:12) still tugged at their hearts.

In response, Paul directed Titus to deploy godly and well-taught elders in every city and town (1:5–9). The main core of the epistle then instructs Titus to call the church to a life of sobriety and good works grounded in the sound doctrine of Christ (2:1–3:11). This epistle is a textbook, of sorts, of the doctrines of grace, covering eternal election unto faith (1:1–2), salvation by grace alone (2:11; 3:4), particular redemption unto holiness by Christ's death (2:14), human depravity (3:3), regeneration by the Holy Spirit through Christ (3:5–7), and Christ's coming in glory to bless His redeemed (2:13).

These doctrines are not taught in a merely academic way, but as the spiritual foundation and living root of godliness, "the things which become sound doctrine" (2:1). Thus Paul wove together doctrine and exhortations to self-control, submissiveness to proper authority, and zeal for good works (vv. 2–10, 12, 14–15; 3:1–2, 8). The apostle believed that doctrine encourages rather than discourages godliness.

OUTLINE

I. Greetings from an Apostle for the Faith of God's Elect (1:1–4)

II. Good and Bad Leaders in the Local Church (1:5–16)
   A. Charge to Appoint Qualified Elders (1:5–9)
   B. Warning against False Teachers (1:10–16)

III. Godliness Formed by the Doctrines of Grace (2:1–3:11)
   A. Instructions for a Sober Life in Various Social Groups (2:1–10)
   B. Redemption by Christ for Good Works (2:11–14)
   C. Exhortations to Sound Doctrine and Meekness (2:15–3:2)
   D. Regeneration by the Holy Spirit for Good Works (3:3–7)
   E. Teaching for Good Works and Avoiding Heresy (3:8–11)

IV. Grace and Personal Directions (3:12–15)

Notes

1

2

3

4

5

6

Notes

7

8

9

10

11

12

13

Notes

14

15

16

1. Verse 2: When did God promise eternal life? Why is that promise absolutely sure?

2. Verse 5: What did Paul leave Titus to do in Crete?

3. Verse 7: Why must an elder or overseer (KJV, bishop) be blameless?

4. Verse 12: What were common sins of Cretans? What are common sins of your nation?

5. Verse 15: Why is nothing pure for the unbeliever?

6. Verse 16: How do some people contradict their profession of faith?

DEVOTIONAL REFLECTIONS

1. What does Paul mean when he describes himself as both "a servant of God, and an apostle of Jesus Christ" (v. 1)? In what way is this combination of titles unusual?

2. Paul stresses that church members should be concerned about what kind of men are nominated to hold office in the church as ministers, elders, or deacons. What traits of character or habits of life should we look for and value in such men?

3. Errors in doctrine or morals are serious, particularly in the lives of office bearers, who must set an example for the entire church. What kinds of people are vulnerable to the appeals of false teachers who would divide the church? How can we protect ourselves and our families from such persons?

Notes

1

2

3

4

5

6

7

8

Notes

9

10

11

12

13

14

15

STUDY QUESTIONS

1. Verse 1: Why are some character qualities and behaviors fitting for sound doctrine and other qualities and behaviors not fitting (1 Tim. 1:10)?

2. Verses 4–5: What should older Christian women teach younger women?

3. Verse 6: What exhortation is particularly to be laid on younger men?

4. Verses 11–12: What does God's grace teach us about how to live?

5. Verse 13: What is the blessed hope of believers?

6. Verse 14: What has Christ done for His people? What does this imply about saving grace?

DEVOTIONAL REFLECTIONS

1. What are some of "the things which become sound doctrine" (v. 1)? How can we acquire them? Who is "a pattern of good works" (v. 7) for you? In what ways does your life "adorn the doctrine of God our Saviour" (v. 10)? Why does it matter?

2. People today are beset with addictions of many kinds (alcoholism, drug abuse, overeating, pornography, etc.). Why is sobriety and sober-mindedness important for the Christian? How can we achieve it and maintain it?

3. What does "the grace of God" (v. 11) teach us to believe and to hope for? What does it teach about the duty required of believers? Why did Christ give Himself for His people? Why are they called His "peculiar people" (v. 14)? How do you live in the world as one who belongs to Christ?

Notes

1

2

3

4

5

6

7

Notes

8

9

10

11

12

13

Notes

14

15

STUDY QUESTIONS

1. Verses 1–2: How should believers treat civil authorities and, indeed, all people?

2. Verse 3: Why should believers act that way? What was their former spiritual state?

3. Verse 5: How did God save them from that condition?

4. Verse 10: How should the church treat divisive people, such as false teachers?

5. Verse 14: What must God's people learn to do?

DEVOTIONAL REFLECTIONS

1. Christians owe duty and obedience to the civil magistrate. What are the limits of this duty?

2. Are the sins of Christians more or less serious than the sins of unbelievers? Why?

3. What does it mean "to be ready to every good work" (v. 1)? Why should we show "all meekness unto all men" (v. 2)? Why must we still do good works? Do our good works have any part in our salvation? Why does Paul say that God's people are justified and made heirs according to the hope of eternal life, by God's grace imparted to us through Christ? What does this truth imply for our daily lives?

4. Paul warns us that there is a danger of taking up questions and topics that have little or nothing to do with the gospel's essential truths. What does he mean when he says that such questions and topics are "unprofitable and vain" (v. 9)? How do heretics condemn themselves?

Introduction to the Book of
PHILEMON

AUTHORSHIP: Paul and Timothy (v. 1), but primarily Paul (vv. 9, 19).

DATE: AD 60–62, being written from prison (vv. 1, 9) and sent with Tychicus, who also carried the epistle to the Colossians (Col. 4:7–9), and Onesimus.

THEME: Brotherly love and forgiveness in Christ.

PURPOSE: To urge Philemon to warmly receive back his runaway slave, Onesimus.

SYNOPSIS

The Contribution of Philemon to Redemptive Revelation
This letter, the shortest of Paul's epistles, was addressed to Philemon, a Christian hosting the church of Colosse in his home (v. 2). Onesimus was a slave (v. 16). Slavery in the Roman Empire was not a matter of race, for slaves came from various races and colors. Slaves comprised between a fifth and a third of the population of the cities. Slavery legally bound a person to serve a master. Their work varied from laboring in the fields to serving as doctors, teachers, and accountants. Some slaves saved money and bought their freedom. Paul called Philemon to not punish Onesimus for the financial loss he caused his master when he ran away but to welcome him home as a brother in Christ.

This epistle shows a warm fraternal spirit, as the great apostle chose not to command by right but instead to appeal by love (vv. 8–9). It also shows how the gospel and Christian love undermined the social divisions that supported slavery by making master and slave into brothers (v. 16).

OUTLINE

I. Greeting (vv. 1–3)

II. Thanksgiving and Prayer (vv. 4–7)

III. Appeal for Onesimus (vv. 8–20)
    A. Appeal from Paul's Heart (vv. 8–11)
    B. Call to Receive the Slave as a Brother (vv. 12–17)
    C. Offer to Pay for Philemon's Loss (vv. 18–20)

IV. Closing (vv. 21–25)

Notes

1

2

3

4

5

6

7

Notes

8

9

10

11

12

13

14

15

Notes

16

17

18

19

20

21

22

Notes

23

24

25

STUDY QUESTIONS

1. Verses 1–2: What terms of honor and affection does Paul use for these people?

2. Verse 7: Why did Paul and Timothy have much joy because of Philemon?

3. Verses 10–11: What had happened to Onesimus? How had he changed?

4. Verse 13: What would Paul have liked to do?

5. Verses 16–17: How should Philemon welcome his returning, now converted slave?

6. Verse 18: What does Paul ask Philemon to do about the loss Onesimus caused him?

7. Verse 21: What was Paul confident about Philemon?

8. Verses 23–24: How do these verses compare to Colossians 4:9–14?

DEVOTIONAL REFLECTIONS

1. How does Paul relate faith and love? How do you give joy and comfort to your fellow believers? What does our belief in "the communion of the body of Christ" (see 1 Corinthians 10) require of us as Christians?

2. Would you be willing to pay the medical debts of a fellow Christian so that he or she could be free of such a burden? Would you be willing to forgive such a debt owed to you?

3. What is true Christian obedience? Why are mutual service and hospitality duties for all Christians? What does this say about the nature of the church as a society or body? How can you fulfill these duties?

Introduction to the Book of
HEBREWS

AUTHORSHIP: The author of Hebrews is never explicitly mentioned throughout the whole of Hebrews. Church history has been far from unanimous on the authorship of Hebrews. The early church proposed a variety of different authors. The early church father Tertullian argued that Barnabas, sometime companion of Paul, authored this book. Irenaeus and Hippolytus likewise defended a view of non-Pauline authorship. Following Jerome and Augustine, Pauline authorship was assumed by most biblical scholars. The Council of Nicea recognized the canonical status of Hebrews partly based on accrediting its authorship to Paul. The medieval church, following Nicea, largely approved of Paul's authorship, and Thomas Aquinas defended Pauline authorship. In the time of the Reformation, the view that Paul was not the author resurfaced through the influential works of Erasmus, Luther, and Calvin—Calvin preferring either Luke or Clement of Rome as the author. On the other hand, the Belgic Confession of Faith (AD 1561) endorses Pauline authorship, and the Puritan John Owen argued extensively for Pauline authorship.

By and large, modern scholarship has dismissed Pauline authorship for stylistic reasons and matters of theological emphasis. Various candidates for authorship have been proposed, including Apollos, Priscilla, and Luke. None of these proposals are without problems. In favor of Pauline authorship is the fact that when God revealed to Paul his mission, it included, besides "Gentiles, and kings," also "the children of Israel" (Acts 9:15), and the audience of this letter to the Hebrews would fit this well. In conjunction with this, Peter wrote to those of the dispersion (likely Jews; see 1 Peter 1:1) that "Paul...hath written unto you" (2 Peter 3:15). This does not fit any other book as well as the epistle to the Hebrews. Nevertheless, unlike the vast majority of other epistles of the New Testament, God has not seen fit to specify the author of this epistle. Not knowing the human authorship of this epistle with certainty should not hinder us from embracing the truths set forth in this great epistle as indispensable for faith.

DATE AND DESTINATION: There are a couple of considerations that point to a date prior to AD 70, when Jerusalem was destroyed by the Roman armies. The author of Hebrews, when referring to the temple service, uses the Greek present tense. While this is not a definitive argument because the Greek present tense does not necessarily mean an action occurring in the present time, it is notable that the author assumes the temple sacrifices are still being offered (10:2). A second point that directs us to a date prior to AD 70 is that the author of Hebrews is silent concerning the destruction of the temple. While some argue that the atrocity of the temple's destruction may have already settled in the minds of readers, this is not convincing because of the emphasis the author places on the temple and sacrifices.

Another clue given in the book of Hebrews is the author's mention of the suffering and persecution that his readers have and are experiencing (10:32–34). Scholars have not come to consistent agreement on when this suffering occurred. Some note it may be the expulsion of Jews from Rome in AD 49 (Acts 18:2). Others attribute this suffering to the persecution under Nero in AD 64. The author of Hebrews does note that his readers have not resisted sin to the point of bloodshed, which may mean they have not endured the persecution of Nero (Heb. 12:4). However, the author's references to a previous persecution may look back to the events of AD 49 (11:26; 13:13), thus placing this work in the AD 60s. It is difficult to be definitive regarding the date as this largely depends on the provenance and destination.

The title of the book "to the Hebrews" points in the direction of a Jewish audience. Some believe these Jews dwelt within Palestine, though the evidence points to Jews living outside of Palestine. In addition, the author makes great use of the Old Testament Scriptures, institutions, and ceremonies. This would easily imply that the readers were familiar with the Old Testament religion, though perhaps more familiar with the Greek rather than the Hebrew language. Finally, there is a brief note in 13:24 ("They of Italy salute you"), though it is debated whether these people "of Italy" were traveling outside of Italy and wishing to greet those in Italy or whether they were in Italy and wishing to greet those outside of Italy.

THEME: The supremacy of Christ over all things and the fullness of God's redemption in Him.

PURPOSE: To exhort his readers not to draw back, but to stand firm in the faith in the midst of the trials they are enduring.

SYNOPSIS

The Contribution of Hebrews to Redemptive Revelation

Hebrews is written to exalt the person and work (especially the priestly work) of Jesus Christ over the types and shadows administered under the Mosaic covenant (8:1–6). In this way the author is making a grand exhortation (13:22; see also 2:1–4; 3:12; 5:11–14; 12:12–17) that because Christians have a High Priest who is seated at the right hand of the Father in heaven (1:1–4; 8:1) and who has made full atonement for sin (1:3; 9:28), they *cannot* go back to the external forms of Judaism and its worship (3:1–6; 6:1–3; 12:25–29) without apostatizing from the faith.

Hebrews begins by exalting Christ as the full and final revelation from God to His people (1:1–4) and as the Mediator of the new covenant (8:6)—the culmination of God's saving work in history (1:1). Because the Hebrews were being tempted by a form of Judaism, which was presumably beckoning the people to revert to the Mosaic ceremonies, the author presents a skillful argument against external religion, and constantly invokes the content and imagery of the Old Testament.

The author calls forth testimony of important Old Testament characters: Moses (3:1–6), Joshua (4:8), Melchisedec (7:1–10), Aaron (5:1), and the Levites (7:11; 9:25); and events: creation (2:5–8), the exodus (3:7–11), and God's appearance at Mt. Sinai (12:18–25). Each time, the author underscores the superiority of Christ over all previous administrations (7:7; 10:19–22). In this way the essence and character of faith plays a significant role throughout Hebrews as the author draws the eyes of his readers away from Mosaic ceremonies and points them forward to Christ's person and work (11:1–2; 12:1–3). Simultaneously, the people of God are seen, in their suffering (10:34), to be a wandering and exiled people (4:9) in pursuit of the great and glorious heavenly city (11:10). The trajectory of the author's argument is that his congregation would see Christ in glory as he lays out the theological and practical steps that the people of God must endure in order to share in His perfect glory (13:13).

OUTLINE

I. The Superiority of Christ (1:1–4:16)
   A. Prologue (1:1–3)
   B. Christ Superior to Angels Yet Made Like His Brethren (1:4–2:18)
   C. Christ Ushers In a Greater Rest (3:1–4:16)

II. The Priesthood of Christ (5:1–10:18)
   A. Christ Our High Priest Is the Object of Our Confession (5:1–6:20)
   B. Christ Is a Priest According to Melchisedec (7:1–7:28)
   C. Christ Mediates a Better Covenant (8:1–10:18)

III. The Application of Christ (10:19–13:25)
   A. A Call to True Christian Experience (10:19–39)
   B. Encouragements to True Faith (11:1–12:17)
   C. A View of the Unshakable Kingdom (12:18–29)
   D. Final Directives for Godly Living (13:1–25)

Notes

1

2

3

4

5

6

7

8

9

10

11

12

13

14

STUDY QUESTIONS

1. Verses 2–3: What does this teach about the person of Christ? About His work?

2. Verses 5–6: How is Christ shown to be superior to the angels?

3. Verses 8–9: What Scripture passage does Paul quote here? What does it reveal about Christ?

4. Verses 10–12: What name, attributes, and action of God belong to Christ?

5. Verse 14: What are angels? What is their mission in our world?

DEVOTIONAL REFLECTIONS

1. The author opens verses 1–4 with at least seven descriptions of who the Son (Jesus Christ) is. Trace them and reflect on the manifold glory of this opening. There is none other who can satisfy our deepest needs or longings. These are God's final words spoken to humanity; why are they such great words?

2. The author continues in verses 5–14 by citing seven Old Testament passages that are for the most part direct speech from the Father to the Son. Reflect with awe and humility on the privilege of listening in on the Father's speech to His Son.

3. Reflect on the privilege believers have that angels serve them on their path toward full salvation. What reasons does this give God's children for gratitude, confidence, peace, and hope?

Notes

1

2

3

4

5

6

7

Notes

8

9

10

11

12

13

Notes

14

15

16

17

18

STUDY QUESTIONS

1. Verse 4: How did God bear witness to the gospel of Christ?

2. Verses 6–8: What Scripture passage does Paul quote? How is it fulfilled in Christ (v. 9)?

3. Verse 10: What does it mean that Christ suffered to bring "many sons unto glory"?

4. Verses 14–15: What did Christ partake of in order to deliver His people from Satan's power?

5. Verse 17: How does this verse show that God's Son became truly human? Why did He do that?

6. Verse 18: What is Christ able to do because He suffered and was tempted?

DEVOTIONAL REFLECTIONS

1. Paying close attention to the Word of God is hard in these days filled with distraction and superficiality. Yet the judgment that awaits those who fail to take heed to God's final word in Christ is greater than the judgment that came upon rebels in the Old Testament. Why is it impossible to escape God's wrath if we neglect this great salvation?

2. What depth of mercy that Christ joyfully stands with His brothers (v. 11)! He not only grants them the name of brothers, but also the experience of His brothers, especially in trials.

3. Chapter 2 closes by speaking of how we have a merciful and faithful High Priest (vv. 17–18). Both of these descriptions of our High Priest are needed. If Christ were not merciful, sinners could have no confidence in coming to God. If Christ were not faithful, believers would not have a continued boldness to come before God.

Notes

1

2

3

4

5

6

7

8

Notes

9

10

11

12

13

14

15

16

Notes

17

18

19

1. Verse 1: Who should God's children consider? What about Him should they consider?

2. Verses 3–6: How is Christ superior to Moses?

3. Verse 8: What warning is given here to those who hear God's Word?

4. Verses 12–13: How can Christians help each other to keep following Christ?

5. Verse 14: What is evidence that we are partakers of Christ?

6. Verse 19: Why did many Israelites not enter God's rest?

DEVOTIONAL REFLECTIONS

1. Verse 6 suggests an important question: Are you a part of the household of faith?

2. Believers have a corporate responsibility to exhort and encourage one another daily. Too often we live isolated lives. How might you help and encourage those around you?

3. Hebrews warns against the "deceitfulness of sin" (v. 13). We often fail to remember that sin is deceitful. When we begin to see by grace how deceitful, how wretched, how awful sin really is, we learn to look to God alone to renew our minds after knowledge, righteousness, and holiness that we might discern the exceeding depravity of sin.

Notes

1

2

3

4

5

6

7

Notes

8

9

10

11

12

13

14

Notes

15

16

STUDY QUESTIONS

1. Verse 1: What concern should we have about each other in the church?

2. Verses 7–8: What can we learn about God's rest since it was still offered in the psalms of David, centuries after Israel took possession of the land of Canaan?

3. Verse 11: What must we do with regard to this rest?

4. Verse 12: How is God's Word powerful to help us?

5. Verses 15–16: How can Christ be an encouragement to pray for more grace from God?

DEVOTIONAL REFLECTIONS

1. Hebrews says that Israel had the gospel preached to them but it did not profit them because their hearing was not combined with faith. The gospel was preached through types and shadows and the redeeming acts of God throughout Israel's history. However, we have even greater privileges and a great degree of responsibility as a result.

2. The word "rest" has a lot of significance for our restless world and restless souls. What makes us so restless? What kind of comfort lies in the fact that God speaks of "my rest" (vv. 3, 5)?

3. Far from being just an exalted Sovereign who is far removed from our situation, struggles, and trials, Christ has a tender heart for His people, especially in their afflictions and temptations. Do you know this throne as a throne of grace in your life? What is meant by this "boldness"? Is it the same as "presumption"? What is the difference?

Notes

Chapter 5

1

2

3

4

5

6

7

Notes

8

9

10

11

12

13

14

STUDY QUESTIONS

1. Verse 1: What is the primary calling of a priest?

2. Verse 4: Who has the authority to make a priest?

3. Verse 6: What Scripture passage is quoted here?

4. Verses 7–8: What did Christ do in His trials? How did He grow as a man by this experience?

5. Verse 12: What should the readers of this letter have become by that time?

6. Verse 14: What characterizes people who are spiritually experienced and mature?

DEVOTIONAL REFLECTIONS

1. Christ learned obedience through what He suffered (v. 8). Though Christ was never disobedient to His Father, He learned from the inside out, as man, what it meant to obey His Father even at great cost to Himself. If sinless Christ had to suffer to learn obedience, what does this teach us about why God's children must suffer?

2. Christian maturity ought to be the aim, not an optional luxury of every Christian (vv. 11–14). Just as children often can't wait to grow up and will often try to do things to demonstrate that they are grown up, believers must set aside childish things and press on in the Word and life of faith.

Notes

1

2

3

4

5

6

7

Notes

8

9

10

11

12

13

14

Notes

15

16

17

18

19

20

STUDY QUESTIONS

1. Verses 1–2: What foundational doctrines are listed here?

2. Verses 4–6: What can people experience but still fall away from Christ forever?

3. Verses 7–8: How are the people described earlier like ground that receives the rain but bears thorns instead of good fruit?

4. Verse 12: How must we press on to inherit what God has promised?

5. Verse 17: How did God confirm His promise to His people?

6. Verse 18: What is impossible for God? How does that offer us strong consolation?

7. Verse 20: How has Jesus secured the hope of His people (Ps. 110:4)?

DEVOTIONAL REFLECTIONS

1. In many quarters of the professing church, apostasy is in full swing. Some change the definition of faith to adjust to this reality; others claim that true believers can lose their salvation. However, the Word of God is clear that many can have the appearance of faith and are not inwardly changed. Let us examine ourselves whether we have simply the form of religion or the true power of it.

2. Patience is not easy for any, and believers are no exception. Yet, without it we will not know the rich blessing God gives to those who in patience possess their souls. How can we take hold of the hope set before us? How does this anchor hold us in the midst of the storms of spiritual life (vv. 18–20)?

3. Christ is called the "forerunner" of His people (v. 20), having gone behind the curtain of God's dwelling. This imagery comes from the Old Testament tabernacle, where the actual throne room of God was located in the Holy of Holies. How does this picture help explain the boldness believers ought to have in approaching the throne of grace (4:16)?

Notes

1

2

3

4

5

6

Notes

7

8

9

10

11

12

13

Notes

14

15

16

17

18

19

20

Notes

21

22

23

24

25

26

27

Notes

28

STUDY QUESTIONS

1. Verses 1–3: How is Melchizedek (KJV, Melchisedec) a type of Christ (Gen. 14:18–20)?

2. Verses 4–10: How is Melchizedek superior to the Levitical priests?

3. Verse 11: How did God make it clear that the Levitical priesthood would pass away (Ps. 110:4)?

4. Verse 12: What does the change in the priesthood also imply?

5. Verses 16–17: What would be different about this priest's ministry?

6. Verses 20–21: Why else is Christ's priesthood superior to that of the Levites?

7. Verse 22: What is Jesus called here? What does that mean (Gen. 44:32–33; Prov. 6:1)?

8. Verse 25: Why is Christ able to save His people "to the uttermost"?

9. Verse 26: What qualities make Christ an effectual high priest?

DEVOTIONAL REFLECTIONS

1. Here as elsewhere the author exalts Christ and shows His magnificent superiority over anything else. Why is focusing on the excellence of Christ such a great medicine for all discouragement and for drawing back from temptation?

2. Imagine for a moment what it must have been like for Abraham, fresh from battle, to receive God's blessing through Melchisedec. Think now of Christ blessing His people after He Himself fought the ultimate battle on their behalf.

3. Reflect on the truth of verse 25. From what can the power of Christ not save? Where can the power of Christ not reach? When can the power of Christ not intervene for good?

Notes

1

2

3

4

5

6

Notes

7

8

9

10

11

Notes

12

13

STUDY QUESTIONS

1. Verse 1: Where is Christ now? How does that give Him honor and us confidence?

2. Verse 6: What title is given to Christ here? What does it mean (1 Tim. 2:5–6)?

3. Verse 8: What passage of Scripture is quoted in this chapter?

4. Verses 10–12: What promises does God make in the new covenant?

5. Verse 13: What does the coming of the new covenant imply about the old covenant?

DEVOTIONAL REFLECTIONS

1. Believers have their High Priest sitting upon the throne. Dear Christian, you have omnipotence and compassion coming together based on Christ's finished work. What an encouragement this should be to you who are reconciled to God through the blood of His Son!

2. Christ is not only supreme; He is also sufficient. Christ is the only Mediator and Surety of the new covenant. Those who seek God's favor and grace must seek it in the person and work of Jesus Christ, not in rituals and rites of religion, nor in the sin-stained labor of their own hands.

Notes

Chapter 9

1

2

3

4

5

6

Notes

7

8

9

10

11

12

Notes

13

14

15

16

17

18

Notes

19

20

21

22

23

24

Notes

25

26

27

28

STUDY QUESTIONS

1. Verses 2–5: What furniture did God instruct the people to place in the tabernacle?

2. Verses 7–8: How often did someone go into the Most Holy Place? What did that signify?

3. Verses 11–12: How did the tabernacle prefigure Christ's work as the great High Priest?

4. Verse 14: What can the blood of Christ do for believers?

5. Verse 15: On what basis were sins forgiven under the old covenant?

6. Verse 16: How is the new covenant like a last will and testament?

7. Verse 19: How did Moses solemnly ratify the covenant with Israel?

8. Verse 24: Where did Christ go as our Priest? What is He doing there now?

9. Verses 25–26: How often has Christ needed to suffer for our sins?

10. Verse 28: What is one difference between Christ's first and second comings?

DEVOTIONAL REFLECTIONS

1. When Christ died on Calvary, the veil of the temple was rent from top to bottom (Matt. 27:51). God was signifying that the ordinances were to be done away with. Still today, we often let our thoughts go no further than what we can see—buildings, people, ministers, etc. However, our thoughts should be on Christ in the heavenly sanctuary, as He is there with His own blood.

2. The sacrifices of the Old Testament pointed forward to Christ, but they could not themselves internally cleanse people. What David prayed for in Psalm 51:7, Christ alone can do through His sacrifice. Has Christ's blood been applied to your conscience? Do you still rely on dead works to please God?

3. There are some who imagine that God gives second chances to people after they die to flee to Christ. Yet verse 27 is clear that it has been appointed to man to die once and then the judgment. As uncertain as our life is, this truth should make us very sober.

Notes

1

2

3

4

5

6

7

Notes

8

9

10

11

12

13

14

Notes

15

16

17

18

19

20

21

22

23

Notes

24

25

26

27

28

29

Notes

30

31

32

33

34

35

36

37

Notes

38

39

STUDY QUESTIONS

1. Verses 1–2: What did the constant repetition of sacrifices signify about the old covenant?

2. Verse 4: Why could the sacrifices by Levitical priests never be sufficient for salvation?

3. Verse 7: What had Christ resolved to do when He came into this world?

4. Verses 10–14: How does this passage assert the perfection and finality of Christ's sacrifice?

5. Verses 16–17: What promises are fulfilled on the basis of Christ's sacrifice?

6. Verse 19: How should faith in Christ's sacrifice affect how we draw near to God?

7. Verse 21: What else encourages us to draw near to God?

8. Verses 24–25: How can Christians help each other to follow Christ?

9. Verse 27: What awaits those who reject Christ's sacrifice?

10. Verse 31: What warning is given to those who reject Christ?

11. Verse 34: How did these believers show the genuineness of their faith?

12. Verse 36: What do Christians need in order to receive the promised inheritance?

13. Verses 37–38: What Scripture passage is quoted here? How is it applied?

DEVOTIONAL REFLECTIONS

1. In the Old Testament, the people imagined that they could do what they wanted and just keep the sacrifices going to appease God. Through the prophets, God made clear that sacrifices by themselves, without hearts that love and obey God, are abhorrent to Him (vv. 5–6). Many today look at the sacrifice of Christ in a similar way, as an insurance policy for heaven, all the while living for themselves. Why won't that work? Consider verses 26–27.

2. Typically, we don't like it when human authorities are angry with us. Consider in this light verse 31. Why is it a fearful thing to fall into the hands of an angry God?

3. "Ye have need of patience" (v. 36). How can the past times of suffering encourage God's people going forward (vv. 32–34)? How have your past trials strengthened your hope and endurance?

Notes

1

2

3

4

5

Notes

6

7

8

9

10

11

Notes

12

13

14

15

16

17

Notes

18

19

20

21

22

23

24

Notes

25

26

27

28

29

30

31

Notes

32

33

34

35

36

37

Notes

38

39

40

1. Verse 1: What is "faith," according to this verse? How would you explain what that means?

2. Verse 6: Why is faith necessary?

3. Verses 9–10: What was Abraham seeking by faith when he sojourned in the land?

4. Verse 11: What did Sarah (KJV, Sara) receive by faith? What did she believe about God?

5. Verse 13: What are God's people while living on earth?

6. Verse 16: What kind of homeland did Abraham and other believers hope to inherit?

7. Verse 19: What was Abraham believing when he was willing to sacrifice Isaac?

8. Verses 24–26: How did faith motivate Moses? How is he an example to us?

9. Verse 27: What did Moses see by faith? How did that give him courage?

10. Verse 31: Who exercised faith according to this verse? What was the result?

11. Verses 32–34: What victories did some saints obtain by faith?

12. Verses 35–38: What different kinds of victory did other saints receive by faith?

13. Verse 39: What did all these saints obtain by faith? What were all still waiting for?

DEVOTIONAL REFLECTIONS

1. These heroes of faith are more than moral examples. They lived in light of a faith that would for the most part unfold beyond their lifetimes. Think of what Enoch, Abraham, Moses, and Rahab might say to you in your particular struggle right now.

2. How is the doctrine of creation (v. 3) a great encouragement to faith?

3. Verses 36–38 prove to us that faith in Christ does not free us from life's difficulties but often leads us into the heart of troubles. As a result the world may judge us as unworthy. Compare whom the world thinks of as worthy ones and of whom God says "the world was not worthy" (v. 38). Whose verdict should matter more to us?

Notes

1

2

3

4

5

6

Notes

7

8

9

10

11

12

Notes

13

14

15

16

17

18

19

Notes

20

21

22

23

24

25

Notes

26

27

28

29

STUDY QUESTIONS

1. Verses 1–2: What must we do to reach the glory of God? How can we do that?

2. Verse 6: What principle can strengthen believers as they endure suffering?

3. Verses 10–11: What will come from the Father's discipline of His children?

4. Verse 14: What must we pursue as we run this race? Why?

5. Verses 15–17: What dangers must we avoid?

6. Verse 18: What do we not need to face, unlike the old covenant saints?

7. Verse 22: What privilege do we have now that Christ has ascended into heaven (v. 24)?

8. Verse 23: What does this teach us about the state of believers who have died?

9. Verses 26–28: What will be shaken? Why can Christians be grateful?

10. Verse 29: Though Christ has made atonement for sin, what is still true of God?

DEVOTIONAL REFLECTIONS

1. Christ endured His sufferings for the joy set before Him. The present sufferings of Christians do not outweigh the grace, glory, and joy of what they will receive with Christ's coming.

2. The author turns the argument believers often make regarding suffering on its head. When undergoing suffering, they often imagine that if God loved them, they would not be going through suffering. He shows how the suffering they endure is precisely proof of God's love, provided they are instructed by the chastisement. What are some ways in which believers might ensure that the suffering, though grievous, will profit them (v. 11)?

3. Who and what is at the pinnacle of Christian worship and why (v. 24)?

Notes

1

2

3

4

5

6

7

8

Notes

9

10

11

12

13

14

15

16

Notes

17

18

19

20

21

22

Notes

23

24

25

1. Verses 1–3: How should believers treat each other?

2. Verses 4–6: What sins should we avoid? What confidence enables us to do that?

3. Verse 8: What does this say about Christ? Why is that important for us to remember?

4. Verses 12–14: How should believers imitate Christ?

5. Verse 15: What principles does this verse teach us about the worship of God?

6. Verse 17: What duty do Christians have to church officers? Officers to members?

7. Verses 20–21: What does this benediction mean? How would you put it in your own words?

8. Verse 23: What does this imply about Timothy? How is he an example of perseverance?

DEVOTIONAL REFLECTIONS

1. The glory of Christ exhibited throughout this epistle does not remove the mundane things of life. Rather it beautifies and magnifies such things as marriage, respect for elders, and hospitality (vv. 1–6).

2. It goes against our flesh to be excluded and despised. Yet, there is no greater riches than to be united with Christ, even if it be "without [outside] the camp" (v. 13). How are Christians in your circumstances sometimes treated as outsiders? How might you be tempted to compromise your faith to avoid this rejection?

3. Christ's blood does not just atone for sin; it consecrates for service. Christ is the Mediator of equipping grace. Turn verses 20–21 into a prayer for yourself, your family, and your church.